Scripta

Volume Four

PUBLISHED BY GISS 'ON BOOKS
HALWINNICK COTTAGE
LINKINHORNE
CALLINGTON
CORNWALL
PL17 7NS

editor@scryfa.co.uk

EDITED AND DESIGNED BY SIMON PARKER
SUB-EDITOR: SHARON THOMAS

COVER: MOTHER BY JO MARCH
CHARLES CAUSLEY'S HAND BY COLIN HIGGS

© GISS 'ON BOOKS 2004
ISBN 0-9542150-6-0

PRINTED BY FOUR WAY PRINT SALTASH

OTHER GISS 'ON TITLES

A STAR ON THE MIZZEN BY SIMON PARKER (1996 AND 2000)
SEA HEAD LINES BY TONY SHIELS (1997)
PIONEER BY SIMON PARKER AND TONY SHIELS (1999)
THE SONG OF SOLOMON (2000)
CHASING TALES – THE LOST STORIES OF CHARLES LEE (2002)
'OTTER THAN A BITCH MACKEREL BY POL HODGE (2002)
DREAM ATLAS BY SCAVEL AN GOW (2002)
SCRYFA VOLUME ONE (2003)
SCRYFA VOLUME TWO (2003)
SCRYFA VOLUME THREE (2004)

Contents

Scrfya – winner of the Holyer An Gof Cup 2004

For an outstanding contribution to Cornish literature

Subscribe and Submit

Scryfa is open to all and welcomes work from new and unpublished writers as well as established authors. Short stories and essays can be of any length to a maximum of 2,500 words. Poems must be exceptional.

Submissions and subscriptions are the life-blood of *Scryfa*. Subscribers will receive two copies of *Scryfa* each year, plus news, updates and invitations to events, for £10 (inc p&p).
Send to: Simon Parker, *Scryfa*, Halwinnick Cottage, Linkinhorne, Callington, Cornwall PL17 7NS
or email editor@scryfa.co.uk

The Rhyme Of The Ancient Pedant

For the attention of BBC Radio Cornwall

I said, "Dad, can we go to
Launceston?"
He said, "Of course we can,
son.
We'll go via Crows an Wra,
It's quicker that way.
We'll pass through Breage,
It's not out of our league
And on to Caerhayes,
It'll take us days.
Over Tregrehan,
It's just down the lane,
And when we reach
Goonhavern
We'll stop at the tavern.
Then down to Fowey,
You'll like it there, boy,
But we'll bypass Lewannick
Where the girls are platonic,
And instead go Illogan
For a nice bit o' fuggan.

Down to Liskeard,
To stress that we're 'ard
And insist on Redruth
Or become quite uncouth.
And on to Philleigh
If you don't think that's silly,
And over Pennance
Where the folks look askance,
Then call in on Dennis
Up at St Gennys,
And pop in on Steve
In lovely St Ive,
Then on to St Keyne
Just to say that we've been
And delight in St Eval
You lucky lil' devil.
We'll see Biscovey
On a nice sunny day,
And arrive in Launceston
Where they'll know you'm a
Cornish man, son."

Simon Parker
Scryfer Carn Marth
Linkinhorne Kernow
Winter 2004

Boscastle

16 August 2004

Anthony Mott

When Valency swelled up and smashed the banks,
Washing half Castle Botterel away,
Did that famed picnic glass at last pop up?
The one those lovers dropped so long ago,
Before the wooing and the cooing had to stop.
And were its shards washed harbourwards,
With cars and trees and broken cornerstones?
Old Hardy would have rued but relished that wet day
With its tumbled wrack and desperate rescues.
Too bad he's dust in Westminster and Stinsford, or
For sure we'd hear those awkward, mordant words
Weighing the monstrous fickleness of nature and
Boscastle's muddy calvary against one tiny
Sliver of glass, in the scale of enduring little ironies.

Time To Grow, Jimmy Bean

Tina Barrett

JIMMY Bean was ten years old. But he was so short he looked more like eight...well nine on a good day, on an extra tall day. In his bedroom he had sellotaped a chart to the wall that measured your rate of growth. It had a smiling giraffe on it with notches up one side of its neck telling you in centimetres exactly how tall you were. Jimmy Bean leaned against it, keeping his trainers on for maximum results and reached a biro behind his tousled red head. The squiggly mark on the giraffe said it all, and he sighed a big, long sigh. Same height as last Thursday. There was nothing else for it. He would have to intensify his tallness programme.

Mrs Bean passed her son's head in the hallway as he hung upside down by his knees from the banister. She shook her head and tweaked his bright pink cheek.

"Good things come in small packages, Jimmy Bean," she said.

With a twist and a flick as deft as a cat, he landed on his feet beside her.

"Why do mothers always lie?" he said seriously.

"Because we love our sons. And besides, I never lie. Tea's ready in five minutes. Go and wash your hands."

But it was a problem, a serious one, and it was no good his mother giving him the old line about small packages because nothing worth anything came in a small size. Take mountains for example. Who ever heard of an explorer bothering to climb a small one? It is far better to say I have tackled Mount Everest with my ice picks and oxygen bottles than to claim to have managed the small incline beside the park with a pair of holey trainers and a flask.

Everyone knew that all the best boys, the most popular ones, were big, not small like Jimmy Bean. They always got the best parts in school plays and were captains of the rugby team. It was like a guarantee somehow. Big equals best.

At school they called him String Bean or, even worse, Half-Baked Bean.

"Hurry up and grow String Bean," they shouted as they kicked his packed lunch across the playground.

"You can have old Half-Baked," they laughed when picking teams for PE.

As Jimmy Bean hung by his arms from the bathroom doorway, he considered how life was rubbish.

Two days later the Bean family were in the car and tackling the long journey to the countryside, to Grandma and Grandad Bean's house in Cornwall. Grandma had had a nasty fall and broken her hip.

"Your Grandma's going to have quite a long stay in hospital so we'll have to go down to look after Grandad Bean," Jimmy's mother had explained. "He's...well he's not all that good without Grandma around."

Jimmy noticed that neither of his parents seemed very keen on Grandad Bean.

But for Jimmy, it meant time off from school and even though he had not seen his grandparents for as long as he could remember, he felt himself warming to both of them already.

The sun was starting on its downward journey by the time they arrived. There was a red glow on the horizon as the family car climbed the final rise to Grandad Bean's house. Jimmy had fallen asleep for part of the journey but now he was wide awake.

His blue eyes adjusted to the space. He had never seen so much space in the city where he had lived for all his short life. Here it was all around him: green, sloping moorland on one side, huge, craggy, granite tors on the other. And ponies grazed along the roadside, their chestnut coats thick and shaggy. If he wound down his window and stretched out a hand Jimmy thought he might touch them, tease his fingers through their coats. This was big all right. Big landscape, big moorland, big space. He sucked in his breath. And it was beautiful.

Grandad Bean was a bit of a disappointment. For a start he was short, just like Jimmy Bean. In fact, Jimmy thought he might even be slightly bigger than his Grandad, even if it was only by half a centimetre or so. And also he was very grumpy.

"You're 'ere then," was all he said when they pulled up in front of the tiny, whitewashed bungalow at the edge of the village. "I've 'ad my tea an hour since. If you're hungry there's a loaf in the bin and a slice of 'am in the fridge. I'm off out."

And he pulled on his cap and went off down the path. Just like that.

"We're going to visit mum later on tonight in hospital," Jimmy's dad shouted after him. "Thought you might want to come with us..."

Grandad Bean never even broke his stride.

"Perhaps he's upset," suggested Jimmy's mother, weakly. "And this is just his way of dealing with things."

Jimmy Bean's dad did something he never usually did. He swore in front of his son.

Grandma Bean was deathly pale. Jimmy thought he had never seen anybody so pale. Her hair was white, her face was white and her hospital pillow was white. In fact it was hard to see where the bed ended and Grandma Bean began.

"I've brought you some grapes Grandma," Jimmy said in a hushed voice. Grandma gave a tight, white smile and closed both eyes. His parents looked grave.

"Perhaps it's too soon for visitors Jimmy. Perhaps you should stay at home with Grandad Bean for the next few days."

But if Jimmy didn't mind, it was plain that Grandad Bean did.

"I've got better things to do with my time than baby-sit," he grumbled.

"Like visiting your wife in hospital for instance," snapped Jimmy's father.

There was an uncomfortable silence. Grandad Bean reached for his cap.

"Well you'd best get your shoes on then boy. Plenty to do if you're coming with me."

Jimmy scrabbled for his trainers, breaking down the heels as he raced to catch the old man's retreating frame.

"Where are you taking him?" his mother called after them.

"Allotment," replied Grandad Bean without a backwards glance..

The allotment was through the village beside the churchyard. It was in a large field divided into neat brown corduroy squares. Grandad's square had a shed on it with a corrugated tin roof and a front door with stained glass at the top and a smart brass knocker. It was painted cherry red and had a doorbell above the handle with all the wires hanging out.

"This is us," Grandad said, unlocking a large chain and padlock. Jimmy was puzzled by the need for such security.

"Keeps the vandals out," Grandad Bean said, reading his mind. "We get the buggers 'ere from time to time. They're not content with shoplifting in the town no more. See old Fern's patch over there..." He waved his key towards another square of brown earth with a shed. "'Ad his brand new rotavator pinched only last week. Couldn't get his teddies in early like he'd planned."

"Teddies?" Jimmy asked, picturing a neat row of cuddly bears all with their ears sticking out of the ground.

Grandad Bean sighed.

"Spuds! Potatoes! Doesn't your dad teach you anything?"

He thrust a spade in Jimmy's hand.

"Oh well, best way to learn is to plant something."

That morning, Jimmy Bean learnt more about vegetables than he ever thought possible to know.

"Now is May month," Grandad had explained. "It's time to plant for summer and autumn."

Together they stretched a string line across the freshly dug earth to make a perfect straight row.

"Now, make a hole right up close to the string, with your finger, just like me."

Jimmy did as he was told. Then Grandad Bean poured out a handful of hard, dry seed into his hand.

"Then you drops two of these in each hole and covers it over again, d'you see boy?"

Jimmy did see and dropped the seeds accordingly. He was surprised how much fun it was. Grandad Bean watched closely and with a discerning eye.

"Too close," he would say. "Space 'em out a bit." Or "That's the ticket boy," when Jimmy had got it exactly right.

For the rest of the morning they sowed broad beans, runner beans and made furrows for two different types of seed potatoes. Jimmy learnt to plant them with the knobbly bits, the eyes, all pointing upwards.

"I'm trying a different variety this year," he told him.

"I planted Catriona last time but they wouldn't answer fer me."

Finally they planted a row of sweet peas.

"Fer your Grandma," explained Grandad Bean as they shared a cup of sweet tea from his Thermos flask. "Them's her favourite. In the summer I picks a bunch for her to put on the dresser every day without fail. She always says how they smells handsome."

They drank their tea sat out in two old frayed deckchairs, enjoying the silence and surveying their morning's handiwork.

All was well until Jimmy asked if Grandad Bean was coming with them to the hospital that night to visit Grandma. Then it was just like a firecracker had been lit.

Grandad Bean jumped to his feet, grabbed Jimmy by the arm and dragged him off the deckchair.

"Time you wus home now boy," he said in a voice only one degree from shouting. "I've got proper work to get on with this afternoon. Got to get everything in before the rain. Go on with you, get off home, yer mum and dad'll be back now."

And with that he retreated into his shed with the corrugated tin roof and slammed the door.

Jimmy Bean scratched his red curls in confusion and started to make his way back to the bungalow. But there was one thing he was certain of now, one thing he was absolutely sure of. Grandad Bean was refusing to visit the hospital because he was scared.

In the car that evening on the way to see Grandma, his father and mother discussed the problem.

"It's pure bloodymindedness that's what it is," Jimmy's father said, barely containing his anger. "He's always been the same, never went anywhere unless it suited him. Mother always had to do the running around and never so much as a thank you from him. That's why

I left. Couldn't bear to see the way he treated her any-
more."

Jimmy listened quietly but said nothing.

The next morning he raced ahead of Grandad Bean,
impatient to get to the allotment. In his head he pictured
it lush and green like the jungles of Africa. Perhaps there
would even be exotic red and green parrots nesting in the
tallest branches. Well, perhaps not parrots but maybe a
magpie or two. He came to a crashing halt beside the
shed. The brown square of earth was exactly the same as
yesterday. Still brown. Still square. He knelt down and
peered along the rows.

"There's nothing here," he complained.

Grandad Bean threw back his head and laughed.

"What did 'ee expect boy? Us only planted runner
beans not magic beans."

"Well how long will it take?" demanded Jimmy,
feeling irritated.

Grandad unlocked the shed, still chuckling.

"You can't rush Nature. It takes time to grow, Jimmy
Bean. Time and patience."

"But how long? How long does it take?"

"Only Mother Nature can tell 'ee that. Maybe a
week, maybe two?"

Jimmy Bean was bitterly disappointed.

"What's the good of that?"

Grandad Bean handed him a cup of tea.

"Well boy, growing – it's a kind of magic, see. You
might not notice anything spectacular happening up here,
but down there – well that's a different matter entirely.
That tiny seed is starting a journey. It's making strong
foundations fer itself right now, developing roots. It
doesn't do fer a plant to get away too fast. I've seen it
happen time and again. Bring a seed on too quick in the
greenhouse and it'll grow all right, but you'll get a tall

13

spindly thing, all stem and no root and that kind of plant never bears no fruit. No, the plant that takes time to grow is all the better fer it, mark my words."

Jimmy had never thought about things this way before and decided it made perfect sense.

"So what can we do now, apart from wait?"

Grandad handed him a hoe.

"Well we can do all the right things like making sure they've got enough water to drink and food to nourish 'em."

He nodded towards the hoe.

"And get rid of any darn weeds which might block out their light and stunt their growth."

Jimmy didn't need telling twice and set to work hoeing carefully along the rows.

The two Beans worked in companionable silence for the best part of an hour until Jimmy asked: "Did Grandma ever help you at the allotment"

He wondered if Grandad Bean might blow his top like yesterday, but instead the old man stopped for a minute and leant upon his spade.

"Sometimes," he said quietly. "'Er was a dab hand at pinching out the tomatoes."

Jimmy took his chance.

"I went into hospital last year, to have my appendix out..."

Grandad Bean seemed not to have heard and started digging again.

"I...I was really scared. The scaredest I've ever been really."

He kept on hoeing without looking up.

"Anyway, it wasn't nearly as bad as I thought it would be. Hospital I mean. The nurses were really nice and I got lots of presents too."

He glanced up at Grandad Bean.

"And...I really looked forward to having mum and dad visiting. It always made me feel heaps better."

Grandad Bean said nothing and Jimmy wondered if he was even listening.

"I expect Grandma's scared too," he said. "Don't you?"

He didn't get a reply but at least Grandad Bean hadn't flown into a rage.

That evening, as mum was serving dinner, Grandad Bean came into the kitchen wearing a tie and smelling of after-shave.

"Off out Arthur?" asked Jimmy's mum, dishing out the peas.

"Thought I'd come with you party tonight," he said, taking his place at the table. "Only I expect Elsie's worrying herself silly in that place. She never was that keen on hospitals. Reckon she needs cheering up, don't you Jimmy?"

While Mr and Mrs Bean stared at each other in astonishment, Jimmy helped himself to extra teddies.

"Reckon she does, Grandad."

On the long journey back from hospital, Jimmy Bean made a list of all the things he would do when Grandma got better and he went home. Firstly he would take down that silly old wall chart with it's smiling giraffe and secondly...

"He says he wants an allotment," Jimmy's father told his mother later on in bed. "Apparently Grandad Bean's been teaching him how to grow."

Six Senses
Nina Mitchell

I saw the earth, touched it, smelled it, and worked it.
I saw and tasted the fruits of my labours, and I heard the
Birds and insects go about their work.
This was Heaven on earth for me, and I felt close to my
God in my garden.

My sixth sense? This is my faith. I believe that in
Paradise I will tend the most beautiful gardens, grow the
Most wonderful flowers, and work the richest soils.
There will be earth in my Heaven and I will be with my
God in His garden.

Jam

From an archive recording of Mrs Puckey

Annamaria Murphy

THEY say that after the 30th of September, the witches have peed on the blackberries. But it wasn't no witch who peed on the blackberries. It was Doreen Pascoe. I seen her. She's been all over Kernow with her drawers down. Causing havoc. We thought we was all safe 'til the end of September. So I picked my bucket 'til it flowed over like toilets on Helston Flora – only sweeter smelling. They bramble leaves was a bull-provoking red. I had more scratches on me than the stigmata, and me legs was swollen right up with stingers. I looked like I'd been to Paul Feast jumble sale. Bruised as damson.

Be worth it for the jam, though. Nothing like blackberry jam to warm a winter morning. Besides that, Puckey jam always got the rosette at the show. Some say it was rigged. Doreen Pascoe amongst them. She's never got over the day when the judges went to taste her pot – it had a fur coat on it as long as Lady Bolitho's. She looked at me daggers then, as if it was me who sneaked in her pantry and opened the lids. As if!

Jam is very important to we. There wasn't much to sweeten our childhoods. Mother gave us tongue pie mornin' 'til night. Father fell asleep soon as he got in. Mother cried at night for...well, I can't tell 'ee that now. Tidn't none of your business anyhow. Maisy Ann, the youngest, reckoned Mother cried so much she was all dried up. Maisy Ann tried to water her once...mother thought she was drowning. She never did that again.

One thing that made Mother happy though, was jam making. We was allowed to stir it with her, watching the thick blood-coloured lava bubble up, breathin' in that smell that was the end of summer, watchin' the skin wrinkle up when we tested it for setting. Our pantry was full of it, and when the last pot was gone...we knew twould soon be spring.

So you see, the preservin' arts was very important to we. When fridgadairs come in, mother refused to 'ave one. Said it interfered with the molecules or something. I bloody got one though.

Back to Doreen Pascoe. She knew all my best pickin' spots. An' she peed on all of 'em, and further afield just to make sure. When the judge tasted my jam, his face screwed up like he'd seen a rats' nest.

"You must have picked these after the 30th, Mrs Puckey," he said. "Jam's as sour as lemons."

Christ!

And how did I know it was Doreen Pascoe? Don't get me wrong, I haven't ever seen her ass, but she hadn't sat down all week at the over-60s. What's more, her jam wasn't sour.

"Anything wrong Doreen?" I say.

"Oh it's just...you know," she says.

I bet her behind looked like father's chair after the cat been on it.

Well, I never got the rosette – first time ever. But it was me who got Daniel Puckey fifty years ago...not her.

The Day The Cup Came To Trescoppa

E V Thompson

TRESCOPPA is typical of many surprisingly large villages to be found tucked away among the china clay workings around the St Austell area of Cornwall. Drab stones, a working men's club – and a chapel or two. Of course the village has its choir too, but overshadowing even life itself are the white waste heaps which stretch away beyond the hills, an inheritance from generations of china clay workers. In other words, you might say, just another working village which has known better days.

But Trescoppa has something else – a rugby football team. Not a run of the mill rugby team, but the best in Cornwall. The small community is inordinately proud of its team. During the rugby football season the progress of the fifteen brave men is virtually the sole subject of con-versation. Almost all the arguments on a Saturday night in the working men's club are heated discussions on such subjects as whether Cap'n Hunkin should have kicked for the line or taken the ball through the centre in the last match, or whether Jimmy Trecarrow should be retained for the next one.

On Sunday, in the chapels, both Wesley Spargo and Harry Hooper, two fiery preachers, might be heard fer-vently calling for divine guidance on the tactics the team should adopt in their next game. The service might end with a call for forgiveness for the full-back who missed an easy drop-kick on the previous day.

So it is easy to imagine the fever that gripped the villagers the year the team reached the finals of the National Amateur Rugby Cup.

The semi-final had been a hard match. It was eventually won by nine points, two broken noses, a fractured collar bone and a twisted knee. All the opponents could muster were five points, a broken thumb, a suspected fractured ankle and a sent off the field for punching a linesman. Everyone agreed it was one of the best games they had ever seen. The final, to be played in London, promised to be even better. The other finalists were a tough Lancashire team, who, so rumour would have it, had included a karate course in their training curriculum.

For weeks the village fairly buzzed with plans and counterplans to ensure that victory would be theirs. China clay production in the local pits dropped to a record low, while old Oggie Williams, the butcher – general acknowledged as being the meanest man in all Cornwall – had taken to adding a free steak to orders placed by the wives of the team members.

"Just to build up his strength, mind," he would say, "Not to be considered a regular occurrence."

There were some arguments as to who would take responsibility for the supporters' travelling arrangements. Colum Jago had offered, but someone was quick to say: "No way! You'd have us travelling in an open lorry while your racing pigeons sat in their loft getting fat on seed that we'd paid for."

A sharp operator was Colum.

Eventually, after it was agreed that any surplus money should go into chapel funds, Wesley Spargo said he would take on the task.

The team went to London a week before the match was due to be played and every day the local daily paper carried pictures of the team "outside Buckingham Palace", "at the Tower of London", and one morning with arms draped about the shoulders of chorus girls from one of the London shows.

This brought forth disgusted grumbles from Oggie Williams.

"To think I wasted good steak for all that gallivanting. I thought they were going to London to play rugby football."

At last the great day arrived. Early in the morning all the able bodied men in the village, plus a few of the not-so-able ones, were at St Austell railway station to board a special train that had been organised for them. They were in a very happy mood, reinforced, no doubt, by the numerous crates of beer that boarded the train with them.

The womenfolk who were left behind had serious misgivings about the occasion. Not at the prospects of the team, you understand, but at the thought of their men being let loose in London.

It was left to Loveday Mitchell to voice their feelings.

"It's not the match I'm worried about, it's what they might get up to afterwards that bothers me. A terrible wicked place is that London, with all those brazen hussies, and their goings on. I should hate to see my David's name in the Sunday papers."

As her David was a wizened little man of about 75, the possibility seemed extremely remote. But all the other women knew how she was feeling.

The train pulled jerkily out of the station and, as the strains of *Trelawny* faded away in the distance, the wives and sweethearts who had gone to the station returned to their homes, taking their misgivings with them. The supporters enjoyed the journey to London. As the train sped through sleepy English country stations, the few waiting passengers were startled to hear the well-sung strains of partisan songs coming to them through open carriage windows, occasionally accompanied by an empty beer can.

Eventually the train pulled into Paddington Station and the supporters arrived in the great metropolis. For some it was their first glimpse of London and the rush and bustle of life slightly overawed the more timid among them. However, once on board the coaches which were to take them to the rugby ground, this feeling soon evaporated. They began pointing out places of interest with all the excitement of schoolboys.

Once at the ground, Wesley Spargo called them together and went over the arrangements he had made for them.

"Right," he said. "Do you all have your tickets?"

He looked around the crowd of Cornishmen and was satisfied with the number of nodding heads.

"Good. Now, mind you give our team plenty of support. We want to take that cup back to Trescoppa."

He held up his hand to silence the loud cheer that went up at his words.

"Don't forget, I want there to be no trouble between you and the Lancashire support – not unless they start it," he added, in a manner that reminded his listeners that he had been a champion boxer and Cornish wrestler before becoming a preacher.

"Now, when the game is over we will meet back at the coaches to go to a West End hotel, where they are holding a reception for the teams and their supporters. After that you must make your own way to the station – and don't get lost. Remember the train leaves sharp at midnight. Away you go lads – and have a good time."

The men broke off and made their way to the various entrances of the rugby ground.

With a wisdom gained from many years organising rugby finals, the officials had arranged for the Cornish

22

supporters and the Lancastrian counterparts to be on opposite sides of the ground. It was a wise precaution. Long before the match was due to begin, cheers and a great deal of bantering echoed back and forth across the green turf. Out on the pitch there was a fine display of marching and playing from a female bagpipe band. Then, to thunderous applause from the huge crowd of supporters, both teams of finalists trotted on to the field.

Trescoppa won the toss and elected to play into the wind for the first half, a decision that met with the noisy approval of their supporters.

Then the whistle blew – and the game was on. From the very first minute it was apparent that both teams were evenly matched and both played hard rugby. By half-time both teams had scored five points and each had lost a man, carried from the pitch. The excitement among their supporters was at fever pitch and it took a few pints of good beer to restore their voices.

The second half was equally exciting. Trescoppa were actually in the lead when they received a major set-back. Their star right-winger, Ross Curnow, was brought down by a tackle accompanied by a punch that went unseen by the referee and linesmen and Ross was carried from the pitch. During the exhibition of high feelings that followed the incident the Trescoppa captain was ordered off for threatening the offending Lancastrian.

The Cornish team was unable to overcome the handicap imposed upon them by the loss of such valuable men and when the final whistle sounded they had lost by the narrow margin of fourteen points to eleven.

All the way to the hotel where the reception was being held, the Trescoppa supporters replayed the game time and time again – and the same conclusion was reached each time. Had it not been for that foul tackle, Trescoppa would have won the cup.

Inside the huge hall in the hotel a platform had been set up on which stood the tables reserved for the teams and various dignitaries from the world of rugby football. In the centre of the platform was a smaller table with a green baize cloth. Upon it was the trophy for which both teams had given their best. The Amateur Rugby Cup.

It was unfortunate that the organisers of the reception lacked the experience of the rugby ground officials. As the supporters entered the hall they were casually directed to tables set around the platform – Cornishmen and Lancastrians mixed.

Their error became apparent during a speech made by a senior official of the Rugby Football Association. He had just mentioned the high principles of the game and was praising the sportsmanship displayed by the players seated on the platform when a voice from the body of the hall shouted: "Yes, but only from the Trescoppa team."

This brought forth jeers from the Lancashire supporters and a chant of "Dirty play! Dirty play!" from the Cornishmen.

Afterwards, nobody could say with certainty which side threw the first punch, but within seconds the hall had erupted into a seething mass of battling supporters.

The speaker on the platform, himself an old-time rugby player of no mean prowess, valiantly called for order. However, when the brawling crowd spilled on to the stage, memories of past glories overcame him. Recalling the old adage "if you can't beat them join them", he took a swing at the man closest to him.

Unfortunately, this happened to be the Trescoppa preacher, Wesley Spargo, who was himself trying to restore order. Both men crashed into the Trescoppa team's table. They went down, swapping punches, amidst jelly, ice-cream and assorted broken crockery.

Before a victory could be claimed by either side, the police arrived on the scene, blowing whistles and wielding batons. The instant the cry "Police!" went up combatants forgot their differences and made a concerted rush for the doors.

Later, as the supporters' train sped through the night towards Cornwall, the rugby fans happily recalled dinner.

"It was memorable," said Jimmy Trecarrow, fingering a bruised right eye. "If only we were taking the cup back to Cornwall with us it would be the end to a perfect day."

Colum Jago, sitting in the corner of the carriage, spoke for the first time.

"If that's all you need then you can stay happy. The cup is going back with us."

There was a sudden silence and the occupants of the carriage looked at Colum.

"What do you mean?" asked Jimmy. "We lost the game didn't we? The other team has the cup."

"Lost the game indeed," snorted Colum. "All of us know that if it hadn't been for that foul tackle we would have won."

He cast a fierce glance about the carriage, daring anyone to disagree with him. Nobody did.

"Right then," he said. "While all you non-thinking men were doing your best to knock each other's silly heads off, I was up on the platform, taking what's rightfully ours."

As he spoke, he stood up and, taking his old raincoat from the luggage rack, he unwrapped it with a flourish and held its contents up to show the astonished men.

"Here it is...we're taking the cup home with us."

The cheering and stamping of feet that accompanied the production of the cup brought the occupants of the adjacent carriages running to see what was happening. In no time at all word had gone the length of the train.

"We're taking the cup back to Trescoppa!"

The police made extensive enquiries, of course, but the non-rugby playing detective inspector in charge of the investigation had no hope of gaining the confidence of the Trescoppa villagers, and he was not the type to go crawling around in Colum Jago's pigeon loft in search of a missing cup.

They still play rugby football in Trescoppa and although they have never again reached the national finals, they do not mind overmuch. They still have the cup. It is not shown to strangers, of course, but if you happen to be in the village on a certain day in May and hear the sounds of riotous celebration taking place behind locked doors at the working men's club, you know what is happening. The men will be celebrating the day that ranks next to St Piran's Day in their calendar. The day the cup came to Trescoppa.

Fernleigh Furze

Jan Macfarlane

FERNLEIGH Furze was a man who knew just who he was. He was the lawful wedded husband of Betty Furze, for better or for worse. Fernleigh Furze was a man who knew just what he was. He was a work-shy, good-for-nothing, pathetic excuse for a man. Betty had told him so.

She told him so as he gazed into the leaping, dancing flames while she swept and dusted and polished. She told him as she fetched water and chopped wood. She told him through swirling clouds of flour, as she pummelled monumental slabs of pasty dough. She told him as she pulled on her wellington boots and struggled out into the snow to calve a bellowing cow. She shrieked it to him as she wrestled with a howling gale to nail down the corrugated tin roof of the shed.

Fernleigh stirred the embers.

While Fernleigh studied the swirling greasy shapes of the milk on top of his cup of tea, Betty raised four strapping lads and perhaps a maid or two, and sent them out into the world.

Fernleigh turned his attention to the tea leaves.

When the primroses struggled through the rough stony ground and the little birds toiled ceaselessly in the hedgerows, when Betty laboured to turn the heavy earth and till the seeds, Fernleigh would cup his chin in his hands and contemplate them through the kitchen window.

But...when the sun streamed through the cobwebs into the little parlour, Fernleigh would slowly rise and wander up the boulder-strewn track. He would pause to marvel at the fantastic shapes of the granite masses, to run his hands over a carefully carved but flawed and discarded arch stone in the quarry, to observe each bird and each flower.

He would make his way to a charmed little hollow sheltered from the coolness of the breeze by great granite blocks, surrounded by the bright yellow furze, where the moorland and the green pasturelands rolled away beneath him to the wide sea.

And there...Fernleigh would stretch himself out and meditate on the infinite blueness of the sky.

Some day, when the sun climbs into the sky, calls you from your bed and fills you with a longing to be on top of the world, gazing over wide, unfenced moorland and pleasant green pastures to the boundless sea, you too may find yourself climbing a boulder strewn track. You may find a magical hollow, you may brush against the rough yellow furze, and your careless stumble may release the exotic unexpected scent of the gorse.

It is then that you may disturb, from where they have blown and lodged among the prickly twigs, the scraps of daydreams, the fleeting insights, the abstract musings, of Fernleigh Furze. You may experience fleetingly his revelations, know briefly what it is to grapple with the great mysteries of life itself, sense transiently how it would be if you had taken the time, as you had so often promised yourself, to contemplate the really big issues.

But even as your mind frames the thought "Thank-you, Fernleigh Furze", the feelings will be gone, blowing across the moor, to Bearah and to Kilmar, until perhaps they snag on a blackthorn, or lodge in a rocky crevice, or tangle in the mane of a galloping horse.

The Goat's Story

Victoria Field

I STAND as I have stood for centuries, the black, shameful watchman of the barren hills of the Greek island of Skyros. I am vile and shaggy, creepy-faced, fuelled by lasciviousness and lust. I eat thorns and chew the knobbly roots of the olive trees. In spring, I hunt down and mount the nanny goats, huffing my rank goat's breath into their ears, perpetuating the shadowy occupants of these hills.

I spend most of my days on the uninhabited south of the island where there is nothing to do but to gaze at the sea, waiting for new moons and a chance to rut. I carry the curse of the ugly, and the clammy odour of the unloved. My beady eyes are yellow and spitefully watchful. I am responsible for all the bad. I am, of course, the scapegoat, God's wretched, rejected one who, if he weren't left alone on the hills, deserves only to be tied in the hot sun on a patch of bare earth to gnaw at stones.

I want to recount a strange series of events that took place on these bare hillsides. One day, when a breeze was blowing up from the shore and the light had a shiny crystal quality, I caught the scent of something unusual. It was a sweet honey scent, different from the dry tobacco-odour of the dark-haired shepherds. These were green, fresh people from a damper, cooler country. I clattered down the slopes, nostrils twitching until my eyes found the source of the sweetness. I watched them, fascinated; five young men in uniforms that were the same dusty brown as the hillsides. They were coming up the gully of a dry river bed leading from the beach to a small olive grove. Pale skinned but tanned to golden, they gleamed against the rocks. Their long legs moved easily, with the grace of gazelles, not in the jerky, jumpy way of black goats. They were men whose beauty made me retch and I wanted to spit my twiggy foul saliva into their faces.

They were talking of military exercises that had taken place that morning and their relief at being free for the afternoon.

"That's the spot," called one, running ahead up the gully, jumping from rock to rock. "Let's stop here."

He gestured to a clearing in the olive grove and briskly kicked aside the larger stones.

The others joined him, smiling. They carried bundles of food, wrapped in bright cloths and removed glass flasks of retsina from their haversacks. They spread the cloths out on the stony ground, securing the corners with little cairns of pink and grey granite, all the time laughing and talking.

The air of camaraderie and unspoken love between the men revolted and attracted me at the same time. I hopped closer down the side of the hill, my ugly goat face grimacing and my bell jangling. By standing in the dappled shadow of an olive tree's grey-silver leaves, I could observe them without drawing attention to myself.

I gnawed at a stump of thorns, as their every confident laugh brought bile to my throat. And how they laughed! It seemed that their conversation was punctuated by warm jokes, smiles and the languid throwing back of beautiful heads. They passed the bread, cheese and olives and swigged their wine, unaware of my presence and my envy.

My hatred was played out by my long brown teeth on the stump. I could sense their soft pink tongues and ivory teeth rolling the bread and I imagined those sweet mouths tingling from the sharpness of the pine resin in the wine that washed it all down to those firm comfortable stomachs. I knew as I deposited my own small heap of goat turds that these were angels whose bodies never excreted.

I moved closer to hear more of what they were saying and to sniff the scented air around these elegant men. One glanced up, hearing my bell. My yellow eyes rolled involuntarily as they met the softly intelligent ones of the young man.

As they drank and gradually grew slower, their talk drifted from poetry to wars, from the South Seas to England. They folded their jackets behind their heads and lay looking up at the clear blue sky. My whole being surged with poisonous malice as I sniffed the air and smelled only youth and intelligence.

One of them, whose beauty outshone even the others', grew serious. He spoke of this enchanted island where Achilles was born and his own love of Greece. His voice shook slightly as he carried on softly. I strained to hear as he said that if, if by any chance, heaven forbid, the gods would want to take him, then this olive grove with its scents of sage and thyme and the warm sea nearby, then this would be, possibly, somewhere he would feel it appropriate to yield his soul. *"If I should die,"* he went on slowly, *"think only this of me; that there's some corner of a foreign field that is forever England."*

As he finished speaking, the wind which had been whispering through the bushes, carrying the far sounds of sheep on distant slopes, hushed suddenly. The sky grew steely grey and it seemed that each of the men's faces cast its own sombre shadow. The white rocks of the river bed seemed to flow with a red light.

I felt the thrill of an impending evil and for a split second my hooves on their dry stones felt as if they were sinking into deep mud. Everywhere, mud and the iron scent of blood. Great crashes and flashes of light cascaded around me. I heard men groaning and crying for their mothers and I could smell the fear-induced soiling of underclothes and the stomach-churning incredulity at being forced to live the inhuman.

I felt all this as the presence of the Devil and felt my power as the scapegoat eclipsing the brightness of those men of youth, privilege and hope. They were young and I am as old as the hills. My presence is permanent, high on my island ramparts, eschewing soft bread in favour of thorns.

The moment of darkness passed so quickly that each of the men thought that they had imagined it. They tried to make light of their friend's remarks. It really was a marvellous sonnet, one said, but they were much more likely to perish at Gallipoli than in this idyllic spot. Another butted in to say, no, no, they would die as old men discussing the war and showing their scars over tea at Grantchester.

The others laughed and I felt the lightness returning. Before they could recover themselves completely, I sprang forward and raced, spitting, through their picnic, scattering their bread and bottles. From a crag above the river bed, I stood watching their discomfiture as they gathered their belongings, trying to joke but feeling uneasy as they sensed that something of eternal darkness had passed in front of them.

As they walked down the gully to the fishing boat that would take them back to the port, each of them at some point turned in my direction and each shuddered when he met my yellow eyes and saw the wind moving my coarse black hair.

There would be pain, chaos and loss. Beauty cannot last.

And so those April days passed with me chewing

thorns, shitting small black shits, shivering and baking in turn on the hillsides until late one night, I was back in the olive grove remembering the sweetness that surrounded those pale-skinned young men. It had been another warm day for so early in the year and the new sage was heady on the night air.

I could see the lights of a troop ship moored in the bay and the yellow tongues of lantern light licking the white rocks of the gully as a group of soldiers staggered under the weight of a coffin. I recognised the voices and faces of some of the young men but their air of gilded-ness had gone. Now, those eyes and cheeks were tarnished by grief.

The bearers staggered over the boulders and then stood still in the clearing while three men with spades jumped down into the freshly-dug grave and deepened and widened it.

The coffin was lowered into the earth as the olive trees rustled in the wind. A *Book Of Common Prayer* was opened and words were spoken that made my black hair bristle along my bony spine. And, when the lone trumpeter played the lament of the last post, there in the depths of a starry night, for an instant, the sky seemed to light up and all I could think was that the angels were somehow accepting one of their own. It was, for me, a moment of pure horror, draining my energies. None of the men around the grave seemed to see it. Their eyes were downcast and tears lingered on some of their lashes.

Frightened by the light, I retreated up the hill to watch the sad procession make its way back down to the shore. The sky was again dark and velvety. Just as before, some of the men turned back to look both towards the grave and into my yellow eyes. As I emanated my own ugliness and evil, I felt my power return. Once again there was the presence of pain and incomprehension.

From my various vantage points on the island, as the loathsome sentinel of the hillsides, I have always seen boats. In earlier centuries, Jason and the Argonauts sailed past on their way to Colchis. Then the thousand ships of Helen spoke so eloquently of the power of love; I was sickened for days. Venetians, Turks and pirates all came to destroy and conquer and the chaos of endless war was exhilarating. In this century, ships went to and from the Dardanelles until Gallipoli claimed its thousands. For a while, the seas were quiet and then came grimmer, greyer boats with their tools of mass destruction. My eyes gleamed with pleasure at the sight.

As for the gully and its olive grove, there were for many years only the occasional visitors who made the long trek from the ports.

After a few decades, a group of men and women came to replace the simple cross with a green-fenced, white marble sarcophagus. I menaced them by leaping from rock to rock, spitting, but somehow they didn't see me. From then on, every year, in the spirit of love, people would arrive to tend the grave and repaint the railings.

Now, throughout the summers, Skyros has more visitors than ever before. Many of them are drawn to the deserted south of the island and to the olive grove. Taxis appear every week, disgorging groups of sweet-faced, pale-skinned people. I recognise them as being from the same stock as those original five friends but they are not so beautiful nor so golden. I watch them wander around the tomb, absorbed, sometimes reciting verse or even shedding a tear for their own beloved lost ones.

Most don't even register my dark presence on the hillside but usually one or two will see me and wonder at the blackness of my coat and the vileness of my eyes. And I will look at them directly so that a shudder goes through to their very core and they feel it all; the pity and the pain, the beauty and the horror.

Rupert Brooke, poet, died in 1915 from blood poisoning from an infected mosquito bite. He was twenty eight years old. He and his companions were sailing to fight in the Dardanelles; a bloody war from which few returned. He is buried on the Greek island of Skyros.

Eleven Men
Jonathon Plunkett

I SIT all the way over there, staring at a patch of mud in front of me, closely studying the way the ruts seem to rise in a series of increasingly turbulent ridges like waves crashing in to Whitsand Bay. I am surfing in on the perfect wave when some overweight and over-wrought Ludgvan defender ploughs right through the middle of the rut. Ruined. The sounds around me are low, distant, topsy-turvy shouts and groans as the night sets in.

It is cold. I'm on my own. I'm sitting on a plastic seat with the rain leaking through the roof above and dribbling down the collar of my coat. The same rain is spreading the hair of the young Penzance defender across his forehead.

His impossibly beautiful (soon-to-be-ex) girlfriend huddles under an umbrella. He slips in the mud and a tubby butcher's boy, who regularly scores twenty goals in a season, breaks away again, miscues the ball and, as a result, secures his hat-trick. This is the reserves losing 6-nil away at St Just. The defender's girlfriend turns away to sit for the rest of the game in the car. She won't be coming again.

Cornish football. Every community in Cornwall above a few souls has a field, posts, and two or three teams entered in different leagues. Go through the play-ing fields at the back of the village on a Saturday and you will find anything from one man and his dog to a thou-sand men, women and children gathered together in any-thing from an open field at Golberdon, Roche and St Levan, a series of grandstands at Falmouth, Launceston and Penzance, to glorified shelters at Mullion, Bude and Callington.

There are perhaps ten people who regularly follow Penzance to away fixtures around the South Western League, celebrating or commiserating in fairly equal measure. It is not like shopping, it is not like a hobby, it is not rational, and it is not even identification with the players. It is more of a compunction.

If, for some reason, I am not able to make it to a game I become a twitchy, irritable, clock-watching ball of nerves. When I do attend a game I spend the rest of the week going over it in my mind...the missed chances, the goals, the small incidents that define the week ahead.

Players get £10 a game for turning out in a Magpies shirt. After petrol, admission, a programme and bit to eat, I am probably £15 down. And all to support a group of sixteen-year-old hopefuls and twentysomething hope-empties and thirty to fortysomething hopeallgones who don't, at times, seem to care as much as we do.

But there are the stories...

Billy Pascoe (a player who never got tackled), used to play for Falmouth Docks in the 1960s with a five-days-out-of-the-water fish down his trousers.

Tomas Lewinski, a Polish seaman who played for St Agnes in the 1940s after losing his way when returning from the war, used to clear the ball to the heavily accent-ed cry of: "This one's for Mother." One day the ball disappeared behind the goal at Lelant Saltings. Tomas, sent to retrieve it, never returned. Years later a tattered and torn postcard turned up at the Saints' clubhouse. The picture, a ball bobbing on some black-sanded Baltic beach, was inscribed with the words: "This one's for Mother."

When Camborne School of Mines reached the Cornwall Senior Cup final at the close of the 19th Century they played all their home games up Scorrier. It was so dark on some days that when the ball went out of play the whole team would don miners helmets and the ball-boy would throw on a lump of ore from the deepest seam being worked at the time. This, rather than any footballing skills, explains why they made it to the final.

Legend has it that in 1897 two bal ponies played for the Cornwall side in the annual clash with Devon.

There is a tea hut at Marazion that shouts the word "tuss" at full volume whenever anyone from the opposition does anything wrong on the field of play...

Often, during a dour war of midfield ineptitude, these thoughts are all that keep us going.

But for all the missed shots and disappointments, there is a certain quality to the sunset when Penzance are losing heavily, that is not present in ordinary weather conditions. The clouds strand across the sky in a series of deep pinks, oranges and purples over the hills, rooftops or sea-views of whichever ground we are at.

Unlike the young defender's girlfriend, we will be back. Because it is here, on the football pitches of Cornwall that one of Cornwall's heartbeats is sounding loud and clear.

A Good Grizzle
Cornubiensis

REAL Cornish humour – whether as pithy put-downs, chapel and funeral anecdotes or longer recitals – is rather like a pterodactyl; it's instantly recognisable by experts, in this case real Cornish folk, but desperately hard to define in simple language. Here is a tale that I collected some time ago, certainly in the pre-decimal era, and I guess back in the 1950s.

Two Gwinear farmers, Farmer A and Farmer B, were standing in A's yard grumbling about things. Their target was compulsory schooling, because it meant that their respective boys, 'Enery and Tom, aged about thirteen, could not be kept at home and exploited as cheap or free labour but – during term times, at any rate – were dragged off to the classrooms.

"I don't 'old with this eddication, bliddy waste of time, RE and PE an' all that stuff," said B. "Better fit they booys stop 'ome, larn somethin' useful."

"Tidn no good at all," A agreed. "My booy 'Enery, ee avnt larned nuthin over that place – I tell ee, ee's the stupidest booy I ever come across."

"Not sa stupid as my Tom," reported B. "Ee ceant 'ardly write es naame."

Continuing in this paternal manner, they agreed to hold a sort of comparative test. The boys were nearby in the mowhay throwing pebbles at ducks on the pond and were duly summoned.

Farmer A began the proceedings. Taking a coin from his pocket he gave it to his son and said: "'Ere, 'Enery, tha's a aff-crown; don't drop un, gose on down 'Ayle and buy me a new frijerrater."

'Enery grinned and started to shuffle off in the general Hayle direction.

"See that? See that?" exclaimed his father. "Fancy thinkun you cud git a frijerrater for a aff-crown! Ee idn no better than a eejut."

"Huh," B told him. "You jest watch this. Tom! Cum 'ere, 'ere's a sixpence for ee. Go down Angarrack, git in the pub theer an see ef I'm standin in the bar."

The boys wandered along the lanes, stopped to pick some blacks and chatted amicably.

"I bleeve my ole man es gone some totalish," 'Enery told Tom. "Ee gov me this aff-crown to buy im a new fridge? Damn ole fool, never said ef ee wanted a 'lectric one or a gas one."

"Tha's nawthen," replied Tom, my ole man edn no better. Gwan down Angarrack, ee said, see ef ee's in the bar – look 'ere, ee gov me sixpence. Thrawin es money round, proper ole fool like. Ee cud ov rung up the pub an' found out for tuppence!"

*

Or, if you like them short, here's an old favourite. A visitor, a busy sales rep in his Ford Mondeo, took a short cut in the Stithians area. After winding round miles of lanes, he found himself at one of those typically un-signposted crossroads; high hedges, no views, no landmarks. Defeated, he pulled in. An aged peasant leading a cow hove into view.

"Excuse me," the visitor asked him. "Does this road go to Falmouth?"

"Mebbe – I aren't rightly sure," replied the other.

"Well, what about that one over there? Where does that go?"

"Ceant tell ee – never bin that way," was the answer.

"You don't know bloody much, do you?" the exasperated driver told him.

The old man tugged at his cow and grinned.

"No-o-o-o," he said. "But I aren't bleddy lost, am I?"

*

And finally, an actual conversation, heard and noted down shortly after decimal coinage was introduced. The now extinct Caddy's tobacconist's shop in Camborne – proprietor Gordon Caddy – slightly resembled a Wild West saloon. Old townies went there as much for a chat as to buy their twenty Woodbines or throat lozenges.

A customer entered, asked for a packet of fags and gave Mr Caddy one of the new pound coins. He got tuppence change, and waved it in the air, arousing general commiseration.

"Tuppence!" he exclaimed. "Look at that – all I get back now."

A wizened old character sitting by the counter, said: "Tuppence! Tuppence! Well, that idn so bad. When I started work, you could go Redruth and buy a woman for tuppence."

Scandalised disbelief, even in the heart of Camborne, greeted this claim.

"Well," said the old man. "Not what you would call a young woman, mind..."

The Bitts

Des Hannigan

He was treading in the long deep, head above water still.
Not quite gone, but easing out the spill
Of the back rope. He'd had his fill
Of the steep, exhausting slope
Of life's last wave, of lost elusive hope.

Yet, through the misted air he saw a burning heart,
The enchanted way of all his sea-spent art,
The shining wake. He'd played his part
In the sea's grudging give and take.
Had sung the joys of each day hoarse, for his god's sake.

In the raw midnight, in the calm midday he'd hauled,
Such times. Reeled back to glory days recalled,
Of the sweet life he'd made on the long deep of Cornwall.
His hands held fast to the shapes of this hard trade,
Held still to every anchor, every line he laid

On built ship and shoal ground. No other way seemed fit.
The riding rope unhitched
On his life's ebbing undertow. The rope spilled to the bitts;
The craft that bore him slipped its final tow.
There is a bitter end. Then life lets go.

The bitts are a pair of vertical wooden or iron posts, fixed to a boat's deck or rail, for fastening a mooring rope. The bitter end is the final part of the mooring rope, inboard of the bitts.

A Meeting At Morwenstow

Michael Williams

A fictional conversation between the Reverend Robert Hawker and the Reverend Sabine Baring-Gould at Morwenstow, high on the North Cornwall coast.

THE first thing you noticed was their contrast. The tall portly man wore a blue, knitted fisherman's jersey with a small red cross woven into one side. His lean companion, in a well-tailored dark grey suit, had the air of a sophisticated squire. Only the fact that both wore dog-collars indicated their parallel calling.

They left the green field and came out on to the cliffs: buzzards wheeling over the headland and, lower down, masses of granite kneeling into the water – miles of open sea. The stouter man with reddish face led the way along the rough path.

"I envy you these awesome coastal views," said his companion. They halted, admiring the seascape.

"This is a day lent, as the Cornish say," said the man leading the way. "Mind you, this coast wears a storm well. Interesting how Turner painted some of his finest pictures in what we call bad weather."

They resumed walking. A sailing boat, slicing the water, made its way along the Celtic Sea in the direction of Lundy.

"You are becoming something of a legend in your lifetime, Robert," said the visiting vicar. There was a hint of the eagle in his stare. "The great work you're doing with these shipwrecks...giving decent Christian burial to drowned seamen." He paused, intently following the progress of the boat.

"I see it as a job that has to be done, part of the vocation. This coastline may look beautiful on a day like today but it's a watery grave between Hartland and Padstow."

The red-faced man looked down the coast in the direction of Tintagel, lost in thought for a few moments. His friend's next comment surprised him: something akin to mind-reading.

"I see Tennyson thinks highly of your Arthurian efforts. That's high praise coming from the Poet Laureate."

"Yes," said the other man. "He was very kind. I suppose my love of Tintagel and fascination in Arthur all comes through in the writing."

There was silence for a few moments.

"Yes, we need motivation, inspiration," said the thinner man. "You need to be enthusiastic about your subject. Otherwise how can you set alight the imagination of your reader?"

He made it sound like half-statement, half-question.

"I have my doubts about the reality of Arthur though."

He paused and watched a Cornish chough fly overhead.

The Vicar of Morwenstow too watched the black bird winging its way up the coast.

"You are probably right, but I like the idea that the Holy Grail is a quest for our better self or selves. In fact I used it in a sermon recently."

They had now reached the isolated hut and they both went inside – and sat looking out to sea.

"This is a wonderful spot," said his guest. "Do you write here?"

"I write letters and make my weather forecasts here. Make notes for sermons and prepare other literary projects but I do my serious sustained writing in my study back at the vicarage. There you have reference books. Out here you have to contend with the weather, though the hut remains incredibly dry. Built it with driftwood I hauled up from the beach down there."

Sea birds scissored through the spray and the sea had taken on a deep blue hue in the late morning sunlight.

"Isolation is important for we writers. I have to shut myself away from all the children at Lewtrenchard, though Grace is wonderfully good about protecting my privacy."

He suddenly changed subject.

"But don't you find yourself a bit cut off, living out here?"

This time he made his words sound like a probing question.

"I love Morwenstow but it is remote and its remoteness has cut out any hopes of preferment but, like you Sabine, I'm not sure I have the attributes of somebody higher up the C of E ladder. I'm not a diplomat."

He laughed.

"Diplomacy and politics...we'll leave that to the bishops. Though I do hope, one day, Cornwall will have its own bishop."

His friend nodded and suddenly switched the conversation.

"Smuggling's good material for the storyteller but a bloody business, is it not?"

His host looked out to sea.

"A very bloody business...murder, treachery, violence and corruption. Not even Mr Wesley could stamp it out. It's several-sided too. The smugglers, the merchants who want to buy, the informers, the undercover agents and, of course, those odious stool pigeons willing to assist either side against the other and I suspect some of the Customs men are not as white as your Dartmoor snow in winter."

It was now precisely two o'clock. Five clocks in the vicarage all confirmed that fact, all at slightly different times. The two men were now seated at the dining room table, a white cloth covering it. Baring-Gould tilted his glass to the light and admired the brilliant red.

"This is excellent claret."

The Vicar of Morwenstow smiled.

"It's the advantage of having a brother as a wine merchant. Claude is down the coast at Boscastle."

"A capital arrangement. And a fine lunch too."

The fumes of roast goose with sage-and-onion stuffing hung in the air.

"I'm glad you are enjoying your food and wine, Sabine," said the Vicar of Morwenstow. He sipped some more claret from his elegant cut glass goblet.

"Do you have much to do with our Lord Bishop?" he asked.

Now his guest allowed himself a broader smile.

"The less the better, Robert. I suppose they have a job to do but I feel bishops are often out of touch with the people. The fact Wesley got such a grip on the people in the Westcountry was largely a matter of the Church being out of touch, out of step. In confidence, I believe many clerics are making the same error."

Plates, knives and forks were quietly, discreetly, removed by two young women, the remains of the goose replaced by plum pudding steeped in brandy.

"Brandy from your brother, Claude?" enquired the guest.

"Yes, and those potatoes came up from Boscastle too. The slopes of Valency Valley there produce some of the best potatoes in all Cornwall. I have a special affection for Boscastle, though some of the old folk down there suspect that, as a young man, early one morning I turned all their pigs loose. I've long been a practical joker but, in my mature years, I care deeply about animals and their welfare."

The vicar poured two generous glasses of brandy.

"Thank you, Robert. Yes, I know of your concern for animals so you'll be pleased to know that London friends tell me this organisation which sets out to protect animals and their rights has strong royal approval."

"That is good news. I hope the organisation spreads its wings."

Both men began eating their plum pudding, each adding a generous portion of Cornish cream.

"I have to go to London on business, seeing my publisher," said the visiting cleric. "But I'm ever glad to be back at Lewtrenchard. London's becoming an exceedingly expensive place. A guinea soon slips away, and in the clubs and restaurants you have staff hovering for gratuities.

"Though there's a certain excitement about London, the theatres and Parliament. I recently heard a debate in the House, but it was not a very edifying experience. Then home again I find release and energy in the moors."

"Money is a problem always," sighed Robert Hawker. "A problem when you're without it and a problem when you have it. Where do I spend it? On the school? On the vicarage? My stipend is a pound a day."

His guest clearly had no intention of revealing his own earnings, apart from saying: "Royalties from the books are useful but the fact is I find fulfilment in writing, especially the fiction."

He tucked into some more plum pudding.

"I like the colour in your writing," said his host.

The other man stared at a seascape painting on the wall.

"I see the writer as a man who creates word pictures. Recently a schoolmaster, a talented young man at one of our public schools, sent me a novel in manuscript form. He wanted an opinion. Was it good enough to go to a publisher? It was an interesting enough tale but you never really saw his characters. One longed to ask is he short or tall? Has she blonde or dark hair? There was not a whiff of description. I tried to be kind and constructive but the man would be wise to remain with his teaching."

He resumed eating his pudding.

"Education is so important. My one really significant legacy at Morwenstow is our school. It opens doors of opportunity for all boys and girls and not just those with well-heeled parents."

"You should write your memoirs, Robert. You have contributed so much. *Reflections From Morwenstow*. I can see it as a title in the library."

The Vicar of Morwenstow chuckled.

"No, I'll leave that to my biographer. Perhaps they'll ask you to write it, Sabine. I'll come back as a ghost and give you a guideline or two if I think you're straying from the true facts."

"I'd welcome that," said the other man. "Some biographies read more like a novel."

"I understand you have quite a number of Non-Conformists in the parish," said Sabine Baring-Gould. "How do you get on with them?"

His host had no hesitation.

"As a movement I detest them but I've tried to befriend them as individuals and families. I was asked to bury one recently and said later to a colleague, 'I'd be happy to bury the lot of them'."

His guest allowed himself half a smile.

"I know precisely how you feel, Robert. Your sentiments match my own."

"Would you have liked the challenge of being a bishop, Sabine?"

"Good Heavens. No! I should not have enough time for all the administration and my writing and restoration work."

It was nearly four o'clock when the two men shook hands.

"I have enjoyed our meeting," said the Vicar of Morwenstow.

"I have too," responded his guest. "And maybe I shall weave some of our conversation into a novel I'm just beginning. You must come and see me one day at Lewtrenchard. Come and have lunch. But I warn you, Grace and I have a fleet of children."

He turned, with a distinctly autocratic air, and climbed into his horse-drawn carriage. Robert Stephen Hawker waved and watched them go up the lane and out of sight. The sun was beginning to slope eastward. Hawker walked slowly back to his vicarage, muttering "*...maybe I shall weave some of our conversation into a novel...* Sabine Baring-Gould, you're a thieving literary magpie."

Sabine Baring-Gould watched the passing countryside as he made his homeward journey. He was in thoughtful mood: such an isolated parish must encourage eccentricity. I wonder what it will take to move Robert Stephen from Morwenstow?

Charles Causley

David Rowan

I never knew the Cornishman
Whose words whisper near
Of hawthorn hedge
And granite tor
And sea-skies huge and clear.
I never knew the Bard
Of the Wicked Moor
Who leaped the streams
And followed stars
To hear the ocean roar.
I never knew the sailor
Whose sorrow salts the sea
Where starfish carol
Over bone made coral
Drowned in eternity.
I never knew the child
Whose songs I seem to know
Those haunting lays
Sad summer days
Beneath the stealing shadow.
I never knew the man
Whose life was surely spun
With copper cord
Twined with tin
Forged in his Lord's Great Sun.
I never knew the dreamer
Who saw lead eagles fly
Across the night
In gold moonlight
To drink by the waterside.

I never knew the teacher
Who from the playground saw
In Willow Gardens
Castle knights
Gallop the forest floor.
I never knew the wonderer
Proud on the Packhorse Bridge
To see the world
With skies unfurled
In the river's flowing mirage.
I never knew the keeper
Of winter in Kelly Wood
Where sunset bleeds
Through spectral trees
And gleams on quiet water.
I never knew the boy
Who ran his race in rhymes
Zig-zagging down
To Lanz'n town
To the beat of the quarter-jack chimes.
I never knew the son
Who never feared the grave
Who knew as true
From Eden Rock
His mother and father wave.
And yet I know the poet
As deep as St Thomas Well
Spring water purls
In poetry
Where he forever dwells.

The Unicorn
Chris Higgins

THAT night, Mo dreamt she had turned into a unicorn. In the morning she woke up and felt her brow. It was not a dream. She could clearly feel a small swelling on her forehead. Oh no, thought Mo, this could be a real problem. Not that Mo minded turning into a unicorn. On the contrary, being a unicorn might turn out to be preferable to being trapped within the human condition. No, the problem, she knew from experience, would be convincing others about the truth of what was happening to her. Others, in particular, being her husband Ken and her daughter, Jessica.

The thing was, strange things had a habit of happening to Mo. Outwardly, no one would guess she was anything out of the ordinary. At best, her hair could be described as mousy, her figure comfortable, her expression kindly, if slightly bemused, and her demeanour... accommodating.

Whereas inside, Mo knew she was a different kettle of fish altogether. When she was a child her grandmother had described her as "fanciful", while her mother used to say she was "highly strung". Nowadays, Ken maintained she was "whimsical", while Jess dismissed her as simply "dotty".

Anyway, there was no time to consider all this, Mo reflected as she pushed back the bedclothes and looked at Ken, still sleeping peacefully, completely oblivious to the fact that his wife was turning into a unicorn beside him. There were cups of tea to bring Ken and Jess, packed lunches to prepare and breakfast to make. For a "dotty" person, Mo was really rather practical.

Mo was so busy frying bacon and eggs and buttering bread that she didn't have time to give any more thought to the matter, though her fingers did keep straying to the protuberance on her forehead. Just then, Jess came grumpily into the kitchen and her morning greeting made Mo check herself in the mirror immediately.

"Yuck, mum. Look at the size of that zit. Gross!"

It was true, it was gross. And it seemed to be getting larger by the minute.

"I think I'm turning into a unicorn," said Mo gently. After all, she didn't want to alarm her only daughter. Jess spluttered into her tea.

"Nice one mum. Can you wash my netball kit? I need it for tonight. We've got a match after school."

Mo muttered an assent and put Ken's coffee on to percolate. She had expected Jess to be sceptical. She hadn't believed her when Mo had told her about the afternoon she spent with Robbie Williams last year.

Robbie had rung up out of the blue. Mo had been really surprised until he'd explained that he'd seen her on the High Street and hadn't been able to get her out of his mind ever since. He knew she was married, but would she make him happy by agreeing to spend just one afternoon with him?

It was not in Mo's nature to be unkind and it would-n't do anyone any harm, she reasoned. She'd always been a fan of Robbie's if the truth be known, since the days of *Take That*. And no one need ever know. Anyway, if she told anyone, they wouldn't believe her.

So she'd agreed, and Robbie had come round in his Porsche and whisked her away to dine and dance. She felt a little sorry that none of the neighbours were out and about to see her triumph, but it was probably for the good. And when they danced at the Ritz, certainly all eyes were on her and Robbie as they swirled and laughed and had the time of their lives. She'd made it very clear to Robbie that it was a once-only though. There was to be no repetition of the occasion, pleasant though it had been. He'd handed her a corsage, with tears in his eyes, and she'd put it in water as soon as she got home. When Ken came home that night he'd asked her where it came from and she told him the truth, but he just laughed and told her off for wasting money.

"Mum thinks she's turning into a unicorn," Jess remarked as Ken entered the kitchen.

"Really," said Ken, darkly. Mornings were never his best time. "Then perhaps she could trot along to the dry-cleaners with my best suit today if she's not too busy doing whatever it is unicorns spend their time doing."

"Of course I will," said Mo, obligingly. "Here's your coffee."

"Don't forget I'm bringing the boss and his girl-friend home for dinner tonight," said Ken. "Make sure it's something special. I'm in for a rise if I play my cards right."

"Oh, and mum," interrupted Jess. "That video I watched last night needs returning to the library."

"Right," muttered Mo, rubbing her forehead gently. She could feel a headache starting just where the horn was struggling to break through. Her lower back was beginning to itch as well.

"Are you all right?" asked Ken, curiously. "You look a bit odd. What's that on your forehead?"

"It's a unicorn horn," explained Mo, quietly.

"For goodness sake, Mo, don't be ridiculous. You're not having one of your funny turns are you?" exploded Ken into his cornflakes.

"No, I'm fine," said Mo hastily. It didn't do to upset Ken, she'd learned over the years. "It was just a joke."

"Well, it's not funny," complained Ken, frowning at

his wife. "Don't you dare come out with stuff like that tonight. It's too important."

"I won't," promised Mo, meekly.

"And for goodness sake go and have a facial or something. That thing looks disgusting. Have your nails done too, they look terrible."

Mo glanced at her hands in surprise. Ken was right, her nails were really long and horny-looking. Her hands felt rough too.

"And mum," suggested Jess helpfully as she swung out of the front door, "while you're there ask about electrolysis. You're getting a bit hairy, you know. Can I have a lift, dad?"

As soon as both her daughter and her husband had departed, Mo busied herself washing up and tidying the kitchen. She debated eating some bacon and eggs but all she fancied that morning was some oat biscuits and an apple. Munching happily on these she went into her bedroom, took off all her clothes and stared at herself in the long wardrobe mirror.

There was no doubt about it. She was rapidly turning into a unicorn. Her neck had elongated dramatically, while at the base of her spine a small tuft of hair was sprouting nicely. Her toenails had followed the same course as her fingernails. She would never get her shoes on.

Mo sat on the bed and thought about what she should do. The doctor was the obvious person to help her but Mo was a bit reluctant to contact him on such a matter. He hadn't really been very helpful that time she had been abducted by aliens. No harm had come to her, in fact they couldn't have been kinder to her, and she'd had a good time with them once she'd got over the initial shock. They only wanted to speak to her for research purposes, they had explained, and had really looked after her well. In fact, she wouldn't have bothered going to the doctor at all, but the strange little people had recommended it would be a good idea to have a medical on her return to earth, just in case the different stratosphere had messed up her metabolism. She'd explained all this to the doctor but she could tell he didn't believe her.

He had given her a thorough check over and had pronounced her fit and well, though he suggested that she might have been overdoing it lately. He'd written a prescription for some pills that he said would calm her down but, of course, she hadn't bothered to take them. She felt perfectly calm and was just sorry that she'd wasted the doctor's time.

No, looking at it rationally, it probably wouldn't be a good idea on balance to trouble the doctor on this matter. Mo shifted uncomfortably on the bed. It felt as if there was something sticking out of the base of her spine. Swivelling to look in the mirror, Mo saw that the small tuft had become a splendid tail. My goodness, thought Mo, things are moving quickly. She'd better get a move on with her chores before events overtook her.

Moving with increasing awkwardness, Mo found a pair of trousers from her pre-diet days that were large enough to accommodate her newly acquired tail. She managed to pull a hat down over her the small spiral horn on her brow and put on a pair of woolly gloves. Shoes were more of a problem, but Ken's gardening boots did the trick.

Not the height of fashion exactly, but hopefully it should keep prying eyes at bay, though she was not sure for how long.

On the bus into town, Mo had a seat to herself on the top deck which was handy because she could lay her tail out beside her. There was one tricky moment when the conductor asked for her fare and she found herself snorting three times before she managed to state her destination. As she got off the bus he gave her a very funny look but she smiled sweetly at him, which seemed to alarm him even more. Of course, Mo thought, her teeth and her nose were growing fast and her nostrils were giving off clouds of steam into the cold air. She left quickly.

Luckily not many people were in the supermarket that morning so Mo was able to do a quick canter round the shelves in no time at all, getting everything she needed for the dinner party that night. She couldn't resist throwing a packet of bran into her trolley even though it wasn't on her list. She managed to get through the checkout by waving her bit of plastic and resisted the urge to pass her usual pleasantries with the checkout girl by clamping her mouth firmly shut.

At the dry cleaners it wasn't quite so easy.

"Ready on Saturday," said the girl.

"Neigh," protested Mo, before she could help it.

"All right then, Friday," amended the girl, looking rather annoyed. Mo moved on quickly. There was no time to lose.

At the library she had some difficulty negotiating the swing doors. She had to resist the increasing urge to get down on all fours and found it was easier to extract the video from her bag with her teeth and drop it on the counter than to fumble around with her increasingly-awkward hands. The librarian looked rather startled but by that time a queue had formed behind her so Mo was able to slip away without more ado. Even so, as she reached the doors she heard a little boy say: "Look mum, a unicorn." But his embarrassed mother hushed him quickly.

Outside in the fresh spring air Mo decided to gallop home instead of using her return ticket on the bus. After all, it was a beautiful day and she really was feeling exceptionally well. She held her shopping in her mouth and kicked up her heels and in no time at all she was back at home, having had the foresight to have left the door on the latch. She'd never have managed the key.

She rinsed Jess's netball kit and put it in the tumble dryer. That would have to do. Time was running out. With increasing difficulty she started dinner, hampered somewhat by the fact that she kept bending over the chopping board and nibbling at the vegetables.

At last, against all the odds, everything was done. The table was laid with the starters, the main course was in the oven, while the pudding and wine were cooling in the fridge. Jess's netball kit was clean and ready, even if it was not very well folded. They would want for nothing.

Mo felt quite exhausted. She swung her head from side to side and whinnied softly to relieve the tension. Catching a glimpse of herself in the hall mirror she realised that the transformation was complete. Gone was the awkward, slightly overweight, middle-aged woman and in her place stood a magnificent creature of indescribable beauty, grace and charm. She was truly a unicorn.

With that realisation came a new knowledge. Not only was she a fantastic creature but she was magical. Anything she wished for could come true.

Nothing could be simpler. With her new understanding, Mo saw that one wish would restore her to her former self and everything would revert to normal.

Ken would be home soon with his boss and his girlfriend for dinner, during which he would drink too much wine and then snore loudly all night. Jess would dash in for her netball kit, demand something to eat, dash back out to play her game, then return to play her loud music late into the night. And Mo would wash up the dishes.

And no one would ever believe her if she told them she had turned into a unicorn.

It was decision time, but there was no contest. With a swish of her tail Mo conjured thousands of tiny sparkles into the air which she used to write a message on the mirror.

"You can only see a unicorn if you believe in magic."

Old habits die hard and for a moment she was tempted to add: "Your dinner's in the oven."

But she resisted, and walked with a slow and elegant stride to the open kitchen door. Stepping through, she moved into a trot, then a canter, and finally she kicked her heels, soared over the garden fence and galloped away – a fabulous, mystical beast under the starry evening sky.

Tideline

Michael Sagar Fenton

HERE'S a naked white ellipse, good for the beaks of cage-birds, or so they say. Cuttlefish don't really look like this, it's just their backbone and their buoyancy locker. They really look like tiny squids, and squirt the sepia artists use...

Here's a linen bag tied with string. Contents: an illegible passport, a payslip for twelve pounds fifty, and five hundred cockles...

Here's the very slate with which I won the Mike and Chris all-comers skimming championship of 1953, the perfect ratio of weight to surface, sufficient thickness to grant momentum but not to sink too soon, until it revolved to a sweet standstill far out at sea, its hot top-side dry to the end...

Here, half-hidden, a shy used contraceptive, care of Mark and Sarah and a sandy encounter when the pubs had shut, soon regretted, another first and last to add to Cornwall's lists...

And here's the skeleton of a guillemot, perfectly preserved by the Arabian crude which carefully etched away its organs from the inside...

Here's an oaken circle, a hammered bung, hastily withdrawn by bradawl to release a gush of cheap French brandy to cheers all round...

A plain gold wedding ring, cast in anger, now tarnished dull as creosote...

A coin, a Spanish real, lost overboard as laughing sailors hurried to their jolly-boats, before Sir Francis' sails could cross the smoking bay...

And glass in scoured opacity, shard upon shard, from

the hoard of bottles Pete and I broke all one afternoon in 1956 with pebble mortars from the shore, as we fled from the radio, and Suez, and the nuclear arms race...

And here a tangle of ropes and broken timber, the sleeve of a boatman's jersey, the arm still inside...

Here's an amulet of Irish gold, set with lapis lazuli, the cause of high suspicion amongst the Cornish porters, though honestly lost as tired cold fingers loaded the galleys in the dusk...

And close nearby a perfect tin ingot, this time concealed on purpose to be recovered later, but swallowed by the treacherous mud...

And deeper yet, the skeletons of a billion trillion lives we call sand, and looking up – the rounded boulders in the high cliff above, and looking down – the fragments in the silt of ancient trees, to tell us there are longer tides than those we know...

And here a mystery object, a rounded chunk of something solid, faded to a sullen ochre, now confirmed by DNA to be a giant, human, bone...

And missing from the above, my heart, which I carelessly stuffed into a bottle before the age of discretion, and gave to the sea...still out there somewhere...

Gwaynten Yn Kernow

Henry Jenner

Gwaynten yn Kernow! 'Ma Mi-Me ow tos,
Floures agor, edhyn bian agan,
Gwerdh yu an gwedh, ridhek en blejyow glan
Avalow yu an jarnow, war peb ros
Savor an eithin melen ol an nos
A-lenw an ayr, warlergh houlsedhas splan,
A wrig golowa'n don las avel tan,
Ha son an mor a wortheb lef an cos.
Re wrellen bos en Kernow! Lowenek
Clewav lef ton, ha gwainten devedhes,
Gwelav gun las Mor Havren, gwils ha whek,
Gwelav blejyow, 'vel henros beniges –
Govi! ni dhre dhemmo 'gan gwainten tek,
Divres a'm bro, neb whekter en Loundres.

Spring In Cornwall

Henry Jenner

Spring in Cornwall! The month of May is coming,
Flowers are opening, little birds are singing,
Green are the trees, reddening in the pure blossoms
Of apples are the orchards, on every heath
The scent of the yellow furze all the night
Fills the air, after the sunset
Which has lighted up the blue wave like fire,
And the sound of the sea answers the voice of the wood.
Oh that I were in Cornwall! Gladly
I hear the voice of the wave, spring being come,
I see the blue plain of the Severn Sea, wild and sweet,
See flowers, like a blessed dream –
Ah me! Our fair spring brings not to me,
An exile from my country, any sweetness in London.

The Ice-cream Princess
Janine Southern

DONNA feels like the luckiest girl in the world. She is the Ice-cream Princess. It is May 1984 and Donna, six years old, is dressed in her favourite swimming costume with frill, itchy mohair cardigan, white ankle socks and blue jelly shoes. She sits on a little deckchair in the back of her dad's van with no thoughts of the Miners' Strike or the fact that her dad had been on the picket line at four that morning because he didn't want to be called a scab. She doesn't think about her mam at home with the new baby, counting coppers to buy bread and dripping for tea.

She watches, mesmerised, as bags of broken lollies exchange hands. Rough-callused hands, scrubbed clean; gleaming pink fingers once tipped with coal dust blackened nails, gently lower the bag through the hatch. Small grubby fingers close around polythene containing shards of orange and white ice that look like fairground goldfish. Donna's dad smiles widely and waves as the boy rushes back to his mates, who are shirtless and equally grubby.

"Cheers mister."

"All right cocker, mind how yer go now," her dad calls, then closes the hatch and returns to his seat at the front. He turns to his daughter.

"You okay babs?"

She nods and licks the hundreds and thousands off a sticky wooden spoon. He starts the engine and whistles as they pull away, raising his right arm out of the window to wave once more to the grubby boys, who are now sucking on lemony and orangey chunks. They don't see him because they are too busy trying to stuff a broken lolly down the shorts of a small, bony, red haired boy, who feebly protests but at the same time giggles while trying to keep a hold on his kecks. When they hear the honk of the horn they look up and run after the van, giving the thumbs up sign and yelling: "Eh, mister, come back soon."

The redhead hangs back, hoping the game will be forgotten, but a flabby kid with buck teeth gets him in a headlock and calls to the others, who resume their antics with renewed vigour.

As the van turns the corner at the end of the street the boys disappear from view. The Ice-cream Princess goes back to her tub of Mr Whippy vanilla, with raspberry sauce, "bits" and fudge stick; no flake because her dad says they're too expensive to let her wolf them down for free. She gollops down a large spoonful of melting ice-cream that threatens to escape down the front of her swimming costume and the coldness makes her chest and head hurt. The gloopy contents of the tub don't look so pretty now that all the colours have blended and she starts to feel a bit sick. Her belly rumbles and protests at its overdose of sugar. She swirls the pinks and greens and yellows into the milky water and imagines that she is making a potion to kill a witch.

The van slows down and her dad flicks the switch to make *Greensleeves* play. They stop in the middle of the road because of all the parked cars by the kerb. The music halts abruptly, part-way through a note. Her dad sits, waiting, glancing in the mirror for approaching customers. When none come, he makes to move on to the next spot, but just as he takes off the handbrake a woman runs down the steps of the house on the left-hand side of the street. She shouts: "Hang on a minute", waving her purse and half-running, half-hobbling across the pavement in stockinged feet. She's youngish and pretty. She has permed hair and is wearing a *Wham* T-shirt.

The Ice-cream Princess watches the pretty woman tiptoe painfully back across the road, wincing when she steps on a piece of grit. Weaving between a parked motorbike and a skip full of rubble, she precariously balances three oysters, a cornet and a pineapple Mivvy, her purse clutched under her armpit. She licks juice off her wrist and vanishes into the darkness of the house. As the van moves off, the voice of the woman drifts from the open doorway: "Jamie! Shut that bleeding door and help me before I drop all these chuffing ice-creams on t'floor."

The Princess's belly growls again and she feels the sloshing and churning of her insides grow stronger. She still holds the tub with the now melted ice-cream, but she's given up devouring it. Clutching herself around the middle, she lets out a little groan as they go over a pothole. She manages to swallow a sicky burp back down, but knows that it is only a matter of time before the dam bursts. She regrets being so greedy. The novelty of being an Ice-cream Princess is wearing off a bit.

"Dad."

He doesn't hear. He's got the radio on and is listening intently, brow furrowed, to some woman with a deep, bossy voice. She sounds familiar. The Princess has seen her on telly but can't remember her name. A woman with a sour-lemon face.

A man speaks next.

"...all miners and the whole trade union movement will come here to Orgreave in their thousands..."

She recognises his voice. He has sideburns like Amos on *Emmerdale Farm*. His name is Scargill. To the Ice-cream Princess it sounds like a baddy's name, but her dad says he's a goody.

"Dad!" she says, louder this time.

"What babs?"

"I feel poorly."

She has turned pasty and clammy and no longer wants to be an Ice-cream Princess. She imagines that her witch potion is killing her, poisoning her. That she is on her way to Heaven in an ice-cream van. Or maybe Hell, full of wafers, syrup and sprinkles. Her dad is focused on what the man on the radio is saying and isn't paying attention to her. Now it's the turn of Sour-Lemon-Face again. Donna remembers the name – Thatcher. Her dad shakes his head, curses under his breath and kills her with a click of the button.

The little girl wants to go home and lay down on the settee with her head on her mam's lap and the "poorly blanket" over her. But she can't. They're too far away from home and still have work to do. She wants to cry. She let's out a little moan and bites her lip. She suppresses another sicky burp, but it's more of an effort this time. Her mouth feels dry but she has too much spit and has to keep swallowing.

"Hang on, babs," her dad says and tells her to get a bag from the box by her side, "just in case".

They pass a woman with two children who is waiting on the corner. When the van doesn't stop the woman puts up two fingers, then drags the boy and girl off in the opposite direction.

"I'm gonna be sick," whispers Donna when they hit the next pothole.

"Do it in t' bag," her dad says, glancing over his shoulder and frowning. "I've got to get some petrol so you can go to t' toilet in a minute."

"I don't think I can hold it in."

He swears. The Ice-cream Princess is worried now because she thinks he's mad at her and is going to tell her off. But she hasn't been naughty. It was him who gave her the ice-creams that made her poorly. She didn't even ask for them. She is not a naughty girl. She is a good girl.

At the petrol station her dad lifts Donna out of the back of the van. Her legs don't seem to want to work at first and she goes all goosepimply. She shivers and her teeth chatter. She wishes she'd put on a skirt like her mam told her to, but she wanted to be a Princess in her frilly swimming costume.

She runs towards the shop, the sick rising up into her throat, choking her. She must get to the toilet. Hand clamped over her mouth, lips sealed tight, eyes fixed on the glass door ahead. The warm breeze rushes past her as she runs. Her hair streams out behind her but she has no time to think about how romantic and dreamy it is because the sick is in her mouth and tastes sweet yet bitter at the same time. She's almost there, just a few seconds more.

She's looking at the door, oblivious to everything else, picturing that porcelain Valhalla that is just beyond it. She doesn't see the beige Ford Capri heading towards her. She doesn't see the driver flinch as he slams his foot down on the brake.

She is still running towards the shop, feeling the breeze on her skin and the vomit on her tongue. She hears her dad shout but she can't turn around because she'll throw up right there and there's no way she's going to be sick outside. She's a big girl now. She can make it.

The car whacks her in the side and she lands on the concrete with a smack, the wind knocked out of her, and she hears herself scream. She sees Mr Whippy smiling down on her and closes her eyes. Her sick, pink with raspberry sauce and blood from her lips and tongue, pools by her head and seeps into her golden, Ice-cream Princess hair.

Footsteps echo down the long corridor. Distant voices ricochet off empty ceilings and floors. The orange light of the setting sun pours through the panes of glass as they hurry quickly onwards.

In her hospital bed, Donna thinks of the witch potion as the nurse tells her to drink her medicine down quickly. She grimaces at the sharp, bitter liquid trickling down her throat. Definitely brewed in a cauldron.

She leans back against the pillow and turns her head to the side so that she can see her dolls lined up on the bedside drawer, and the handmade card from her school friends, with its message: "Dear Donna, Get well soon, Lots of love, Class 2B." Followed by thirty kisses.

As she turns, she sees them coming towards her: her mam, dad and baby sister. They look worried but they're smiling. She smiles back. Her mam sits on the edge of the bed and kisses her. Her dad reaches into his pocket and pulls out a twisted paper bag.

"'Ere you go, Babs. I got you some spice*."

She untwists the bag and digs out a pink shrimp. She is the luckiest girl in the world.

---

* Spice is colloquial for sweets in Yorkshire

At Sharrow Grot

Joseph Lugger

Look round, on this terraqueous ball,
How all the nations rise and fall;
In wisdom's scales, clear is the case,
Prudence exalts as wiles abase;
By ill-judged measures, Britain see!
America no more depends on thee.

The Wooden Cubes

Colin Wilson

O N my desk as I write there are two black wooden cubes, about an inch each way. They are connected with one of the strangest stories I have ever heard. About two years ago, as I was walking through a back street in Soho, I discovered a tiny second-hand shop. The old man who kept the shop was a bent little creature called Masun. I discovered a copy of Laver's excellent volume on Nostradamus and bought it. This led us into a conversation about the great French prophet of the future.

It turned out that Masun was also fascinated by him. How could Nostradamus, who died in 1566, have predicted with such terrible accuracy the exact date of the French Revolution two centuries later? How, in fact, is it possible to foresee the future?

As we talked, I noticed a number of people who walked through the shop and went upstairs. Masun explained to me that these were the chinos of Madame Margot, an old fortune-teller who rented a room from him.

Masun and I became firm friends. I dropped in to see him at least once a week. One morning when I called, the place was in an uproar. Madame Margot had just died of a heart attack. I decided not to add to the confusion, so I sneaked off, promising to return two weeks later, when I returned from a trip to Cornwall searching for ancient manuscripts.

In fact my trip lasted a month. When I returned, I was horrified to find that the shop was now being drastically altered. One of the workmen told me it was being turned into a coffee bar. After various enquiries I discovered that Masun had suffered a stroke and was in hospital at Windsor.

Late that afternoon – a damp, misty autumn day – I was in his room at the hospital. I was shocked by the change in my old friend. He was like a collapsed balloon. Finally, as the dusk turned to darkness, he told me the amazing story that I now set down.

Madame Margot died very suddenly. The doctor who examined her reported that the poor old creature was half-starved. She owed Masun over a hundred pounds.

He was a good-natured old soul. Rather than allow her to be buried in a pauper's grave he paid for a cheap funeral out of his own savings. And after her funeral he started to clear out her room. One of the first things he found was a polished black wooden cube. It fascinated him. It was very smooth and icy cold to the touch. Finally he discovered its mate at the back of a drawer.

It was now that he received his first shock. Naturally, he held the cubes side by side. Immediately they drew together as if they had magnets concealed inside them.

Examining them more closely, he was amazed by their smoothness. They were made of wood – mahogany, or stained oak.

Masun was puzzled. He slipped them into his pocket, and took them out occasionally to gaze at them. So it happened that, later the same day, he was sitting in his shop, holding the cubes, when his nephew came in with a pretty girl. He introduced the girl as his future wife. A few minutes later he slipped over to Masun, and whispered proudly: "Don't you think she'll make a good wife?"

Masun looked across the room at the girl, still holding the cubes. And then the strange thing happened.

Masun said: "It was as though the cubes turned to fire in my hand."

Quite suddenly, he said, all his faculties seemed to concentrate and he was able to foresee the future. With terrible clarity, he realised that the girl would not live to be married. As he looked at her, it was as if she was already involved in the street accident that would kill her.

For twenty-four hours, he told me, he thought that he would go insane; the burden of this knowledge was too horrible for an old man.

Then, luckily, he began to wonder about the properties of the two cubes. He discovered a passage in the *Necronomican* of the mad Arab Abdul Lurens that mentioned the possibility of divination by means of cubes cut from the wood of the Arabian gum tree.

A young poet came into his shop while he was reading, and told him a gloomy story of rejections by thirty publishers. Gripping the wooden cubes, he was suddenly aware that the poet was destined to be a future Nobel Prize winner.

This cheered him up. Obviously, there was a positive side to this business of knowing the future. And in fact he spoke so encouragingly that the poet left the shop declaring that he would try just one more publisher.

Masun realised that he possessed a secret that could be of inestimable value to mankind.

And then, a few days later, he discovered a new property of the cubes – his most exciting discovery yet. It happened that he was standing in the window of his shop staring out along the street. His attention suddenly became fixed on a thin, exhausted-looking woman who was pushing a pram. Something about her troubled him.

He reached into his pocket and touched the cubes. Immediately he realised with horror what disturbed him about her. It was her nearness to tragedy.

Even as he watched, feeling his faculties concentrate strangely as the strength flexed along his arm, she turned the pram and started to push it into the road.

At that moment a taxi swerved out of a side street. A second before it happened Masun could already hear the crunching of the wood as the taxi ground the pram against the lamppost.

And yet the sense of power emanating from the cubes made it impossible for him to feel overwhelmed by the prospect. His mind seemed to make a new effort of concentration.

The taxi and the woman blurred – as if they turned into a kind of jelly, he told me. And then the taxi had come to a standstill within a foot of the pram.

And Masun knew with absolute certainty that the cubes had given him the power to alter the future as well as to know it.

That night, he felt terribly exhausted. And yet he knew that he had a mission. He now held power in his hands. But he knew nothing about it. He took from his shelves all his volumes on magic.

Only one writer – Gurdjieff – had a curious paragraph that seemed to go to the point. Its essence was this: some people have a destiny; others happen according to chance.

But the woman's baby had been destined to be killed and he had somehow been able to prevent it.

That made Masun very excited. One of his most shattering memories was Chamberlain's declaration of war in 1939. He could perhaps even have prevented Hitler giving the orders that started the march into Poland.

Masun was not very interested in politics. But he was a very public-spirited man, and now his duty seemed plain. He must study politics carefully, use his powers of foreseeing the future and then use the cubes to alter the future at some crucial point.

He began to study the newspapers every morning. And on the second day, he read of an event which excited him.

His paper merely reported that a certain Eastern prime minister was paying a visit to London to discuss trade relations.

Instantly, with his power of foresight, Masun knew that this was not the true reason, and that the results of these two talks would be disastrous for at least two Central European countries.

Twenty-four hours later Masun was waiting at London Airport for the arrival of the plane. Waiting beside him at the barrier was a certain important member of the British Cabinet who Masun recognised.

He smiled to himself. The Cabinet Minister was unaware that his important guest would trip on the gangway and seriously injure his leg. But Masun was aware, for he had the thing planned.

The plane stopped on the runway and slowly taxied towards the customs building. The gangway was lowered. The first person to appear was the prime minister.

Masun watched him take a step forward, clutched the cubes and willed the gangway to move away from the plane.

Then he realised his mistake. It felt, he said, as if he had fallen over the Niagara Falls. Some immense power seemed to catch him and sweep him away. He felt a sharp pain in his chest, gave a cry and collapsed.

A week later when he woke up in hospital he learned that he had had two serious haemorrhages.

After that, he had himself transferred to the Windsor hospital where I spoke to him. He told me that he knew he was a dying man.

But what happened at the airport? He could only make a guess. Somehow, he felt he was interfering with some immense force of history. He had been able to interfere in the minor destiny of a woman pushing a pram because it was like changing the course of a small stream.

But this time he had tried to change the course of some huge river and the effort wrecked him.

I shuddered as I heard his words, thinking of all their implications.

I spent many hours with Masun in the last months of his life. He died before Christmas and made me a present of the two cubes.

I have forgotten to mention one strange result of his final experience at the airport. The cubes became slightly warped, like metal that has been in a fire. Their sides no longer fitted together.

And as I press them together now, on my desk, they are as indifferent to one another as any other two pieces of carved wood.

Strange. But as I touched them just now, I felt a distinct shock. But no, it is impossible.

Notes On The Contributors

Tina Barrett lives and writes at the foot of Kit Hill. Her book, *The Bal-Maiden's Boy*, was runner-up for the 2002 WHSmith Raw Talent Award. She is currently concentrating on a book for children, *The Silver-Spoked Wheel*, and Hodder is publishing one of her stories in its *Midnight Library* series.

Cornubiensis is the pen-name of a Camborne man who has been collecting local sayings and stories all his life; he writes and publishes extensively, but, as he says, "on far less exciting topics".

Victoria Field was born in 1963 and has lived and worked in Russia, Pakistan and Cornwall. She has won numerous prizes, including the Bloc Online prize at Falmouth Literary Festival 2004. She is training to be a poetry therapist. A major collection, *Olga's Dreams*, is published by fal (www.falpublications.co.uk).

Des Hannigan lives in Morvah, and is a writer and photographer who works mainly on travel guidebooks. He has written guides to Northern Europe, Denmark, Ireland, Andalucía, Greece and North Pakistan. His latest book, *Eccentric Britain*, was published by New Holland in October 2004. In a previous life he was a fisherman.

Chris Higgins was born in South Wales, and her grandfather was from Launceston. She has taught English in Penwith schools for 25 years. She is now concentrating on her writing and has written a novel for teenagers, *Boobs*, and a number of short stories. She is currently writing her second novel.

Henry Jenner (1848-1934) is regarded as the father of the modern Cornish language movement, and 2004 marks the centenary of the publication of his *Handbook Of The Cornish Language*, which helped accelerate the revival of the tongue. He helped Cornwall gain acceptance as a Celtic nation by the Pan-Celtic Congress, founded the Old Cornwall Society and was the first Grand Bard of the Gorsedd. *Henry And Katharine Jenner – A Celebration Of Cornwall's Culture, Language And Identity* is published by Francis Boutle.

Joseph Lugger was born at Cawsand in 1726. After serving with His Majesty's Navy he made his home in a small cave at Sharrow Grot, between Freathy and Tregantle Fort. His erudite verses are still visible where he carved them into the stone roof. Lugger died in 1798.

Jan Macfarlane was born and grew up on the banks of Loch Lomond, close to where her ancestors had, for generations, made their living from stealing cattle. She has lived in Cornwall for a quarter of a century, working as a doctor, raising some children, gardening, and writing.

Jo March was born in 1962, the daughter of a farmer and a district nurse. She grew up in the small moorland village of Darite, in South East Cornwall. A self-taught painter, her inspiration is drawn from her environment and the people that inhabited her childhood. She has a fascination with the eccentricities which exist just below the surface of Cornish rural life. Her work is exhibited in Cornwall, Dorset and Worcestershire, and she also undertakes greyhound and lurcher portrait commissions.

Nina Mitchell was born in Italy in 1947. She was educated in Cornwall where she worked and eventually married. She has a grown-up son and now lives with her family in Wiltshire. She likes to write and is currently working on a collection of children's stories set in Cornwall.

Anthony Mott republished twenty outstanding works in his *Cornish Library* series during the 1980s. He has lectured at the Daphne du Maurier festival at Fowey on 'Q', Thomas Hardy, Geoffrey Grigson, Virginia Woolf and Charles Causley. He has lived at St Merryn, Withiel, Zennor and Mousehole, but now lives in London.

Annamaria Murphy writes for Scavel An Gow, Kneehigh, Alibi, Brainstorm Films, The Eden Project, and almost anyone who will have her. She wrote for Kneehigh's *Tristan and Iseult*, and *The Bacchae* and is currently writing *The Visitation Of Roberto Collioni* for Platform 4. She lives in Paul with her daughter Georgia.

Jonathon Plunkett grew up in Penzance. In 1972 he saw his first match at Penlee Park and has supported Penzance AFC ever since. He studied Theatre at Lancaster University, worked as an actor, trained as a drama teacher, and returned to Cornwall to work at Callington Community College, where he teaches, writes, acts and directs.

David Rowan was born in Cornwall and has lived all his life at Fowey. He teaches English at Bodmin College, where he enjoys the opportunity to introduce students to the poetry of Charles Causley and the work of other Cornish writers.

Michael Sagar Fenton is a Penzance-born writer and columnist, whose day jobs have included record shop owner, actor, zoo-keeper, estate agent and dairy farmer. He acts as public relations officer for Penlee Lifeboat. His published work includes *Penlee: The Loss Of A Lifeboat* and *Rosebud And The Newlyn Clearances*.

Janine Southern is the daughter of a coal miner, and was born and raised in Castleford, West Yorkshire. At the age of five she ate regularly in the Miners' Welfare soup kitchens. She studied drama at Exeter University and now lives at St Ive Keason, in the shadow of Caradon Hill. She works in Looe and Liskeard schools.

E V Thompson was born in London and served in the

Navy and with Bristol police. In 1977 *Chase the Wind* won the Best Historic Novelist Award. He followed this with a host of titles, including *Ben Retallick, Harvest Of The Sun*, and *Music Makers*. His latest novel, *Tomorrow Is For Ever* was published in November 2004. He is a Bard of the Gorsedd and lives at Pentewan.

Michael Williams is a writer and Bard of the Gorsedd. A Cornishman, he founded Bossiney Books and was in publishing for 25 years. He lives near St Teath where he continues to write and operate as a publishing and writing consultant.

Colin Wilson was born in Leicester in 1931. His first book, *The Outsider*, was published by Victor Gollancz in 1956 to universal acclaim and he was dubbed, along with John Osborne, the original "Angry Young Man". Many books followed this success and in 1971 *The Occult* gave him a new, worldwide audience. He has lived in Cornwall for more than forty years. An autobiography, *Dreaming To Some Purpose*, has just been published.